Praise for
REALITY AND THE POSITIVE POWER OF PERSPECTIVE

"When I began reading RATPPOP, I figured, "I know all about this stuff." Well, turns out, I didn't, and the additions the book made to my already-passionate-positive-energetic mindset were welcome. The perspectives of Personal, Shared, and Collective reality generated empowering thoughts. The concept of taking action immediately is obvious, but oh-so-elusive in our comfort zone. I've written my Magic List, and merely seeing it on a page is already generating excitement about seeing it come to fruition. The reminder of gut-instinct is important in so many ways.

Aaron's book came to me on a morning when reading it was the best thing I could have hoped for. A welcome chapter in Life's book of self-help."

— *Roger Fisher*
Founding Member of Heart
and Rock & Roll Hall of Fame Inductee

"This book on the positive power of perspective is a wonderful read and workbook with action exercises and delightful illustrations throughout. Aaron lets the reader see how perception is the key to all experiences, and the Three Realities help us choose how we live our lives! His life coaching experience leads us to take action on practicing mindfulness and living in the moment of each experience. As he writes, 'Life isn't happening to you. You are creating it'. Great work!"

— *Starlyn Cooper* A.S., B.S, M.ED, CCRC
Master Resiliency Trainer for the United States Air Force

"Aaron Bethune has written a delightful and generous book. Read, reflect, revitalize."

— *Marty Neumeier*
Author of *Metaskills, The Brand Gap,* ZAG

"For those who look at life from their own perspective and struggle to achieve their goals — this is the book that will alter perspective... and open the door to achievement."
— *Cathleen McMahon*
Chief Executive Officer of Mission Management Group

"*Reality and The Positive Power of Perspective* works to remind me to be mindful of zooming out enough to see my life in perspective. Reflecting upon the Personal, Collective and Shared realities that I can perceive from where I am."
— *Bob Guido*
Composer & Producer

"This book is a treasure map that leads us to our own method of thought as the key to unlock the treasures of life. Now more than ever this should be taught in schools across the globe."
— *Chief Dana Tizya-Tramm*

"Perspective plays a big role in how you experience life and the reality you live. Often, before you can live differently, you must first see differently. Some books have the power to change how you see the world — this is one of them."
— *Dez Dickerson*
Prince and the Revolution

"What I love most about RATPPOP is that while the topic of perceiving one's own reality can be a deep or even heavy one, Aaron Bethune makes it an enjoyable, casual conversation. With short, but meaningful chapters and wonderfully engaging illustrations along the way, RATPPOP leaves you with plenty to not only think about, but specific steps and suggestions on how create and enjoy your own personal reality at a more intentional and fulfilling level.

— *Ryan Stanley*
Professional Life Coach

*Dedicated to my four seasons:
Laura, Oliver, Julie, and Celeste.*

Reality and the positive power of -perspective-

a book by
aaron bethune

© Aaron Bethune 2020. All rights reserved.

No part of this book may be used or reproduced in any manner whatsoever without the express written permission of the publisher or author. The exception would be in the case of brief quotations embodied in critical articles or reviews, and pages where permission is specifically granted by the publisher or author, or in the case of photocopying, a licence from Access Copyright, www.accesscopyright.ca, 1-800-893-5777, info@accesscopyright.ca.

Library of Canada Cataloguing in Publication data is available.

ISBN 978-0-9936367-5-2 (Hardcover Edition)
ISBN 978-1-9895280-4-4 (Paperback Edition)
ISBN 978-0-9936367-7-6 (E-book Edition)
ISBN 978-0-9936367-8-3 (Audiobook Edition)

First Edition Printing 2020

Front cover image, illustrations, and hand-lettering
by Laura Lavender
Book design by Clint Hutzulak

Published in Canada by Above the Noise, Victoria, BC
www.abovethenoisepublishing.com.

For more information contact: publishing@abovethenoise.ca

Special discounts are available on quantity purchases by corporations, associations, and others. For details, contact the publisher at the address above.

For more information on the book and author please visit www.aaronbethune.com

Reality
and
the positive
power
of
- perspective -

a book by
aaron bethune

Published by

CONTENTS

- 5 Prologue
- 9 The Three Realities
- 33 Does Consciousness Create the Universe?
- 39 Putting It into Perspective
- 43 Alone Together
- 45 What Is, Is and What Will Be, Is Not
- 49 The Power of Words
- 57 Communicating Openly
- 61 That's My Story, and I'm Sticking to It!
- 65 Manifesting your Personal Reality
- 73 Leaving Your Comfort Zone
- 77 Taking Action
- 81 Metamorphosis
- 95 Frustration
- 99 Judgment
- 103 Anger & Blame
- 107 Mindfulness
- 115 Meaning
- 121 Finding Flow
- 125 Focus
- 127 Your Magic List
- 133 Thoughts & Actions to Live By
- 139 Epilogue
- 143 Acknowledgments
- 145 About the author

Granddaughter: *"How long have we been waiting for the bus? It feels like forever!"*
Grandmother: *"Oh, only about 5 minutes."*

PROLOGUE

My friends and family will tell you that my favourite word, or at least one of them, is *perspective*. It's a powerful word because to me it represents the key to happiness and success in life. Which may help explain why I ended up writing this little book.

If we circle an object and see it from different points of view, what has changed is our position. However, neither the object nor ourselves have changed. And if two people are standing side by side, one joyfully celebrating a birthday and the other having just lost a grandfather, the weather may be beautiful, but the perspective the two have of the day is likely very different. So it is our internal thoughts that determine how we perceive what we experience. If we can change our thoughts, we can change our perspectives and consequently our experiences.

We can view any of the circumstances in our lives from a potentially infinite number of perspectives. If we don't like the first perspective that presents itself, we can try to find another. Humour can help, especially when it comes to examining the harder things in life. Sometimes finding a new perspective can be incredibly difficult. Notice I didn't say

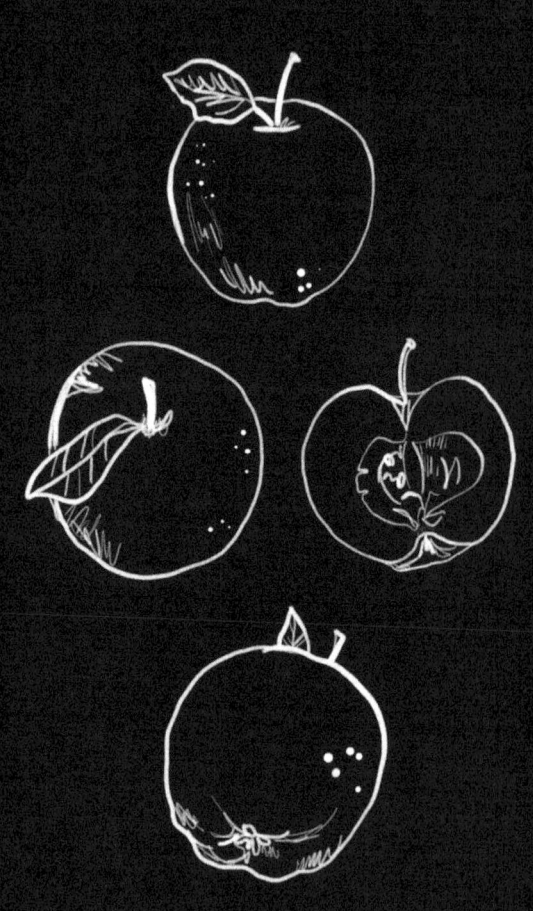

impossible! Sooner or later we can look back on anything and see it in a different light. Some things can take a long time to see differently. A good trick, it seems, is to be able to reduce the amount of time it takes to see a new perspective, and something that can help with that is being aware that changing perspectives is entirely possible in real time.

Perspective is the key to how we react to all experiences. This little book intertwines thoughts about perspectives with thoughts about reality, and I hope it can help provide another perspective to what you are experiencing in your life right now. My perspective on reality may not be totally original to every reader, but I hope every reader is better off for considering the ideas to be discussed. Note too that in describing this, I am setting aside all thoughts about different spiritual belief systems — think of this as a secular book!

> **ACTION:** *As I was writing, a few people asked me, "How will I put this information to work for me?" A concise and practical list of steps 1 through 10 would be ideal for many. The problem is, everybody is different, and there is no universal list. So instead I have sprinkled specific suggestions labelled as "Actions" throughout the book, in the hope that every reader will be able to find at least a few practical pointers to act on.*

THE THREE REALITIES

It can take years to realize that we don't all experience things the same way. In my own life, I was on a ferry when it first hit me that all I know of reality is my own unique experience. That thought quickly developed into a way of looking at things that has helped me view everything in my life differently, something I will share here. Using the lens of what I have called the "**three realities**" is simply a perspective on reality that can be used as a tool. Those realities are:

#1. **Personal Reality**
#2. **Shared Reality**
#3. **Collective Reality**

Or, to put it another way: **Me**, **You + Me**, and **All of Us**.

Personal Reality is our observer's view, our unique perspective on life. What we deem to be outside of our Personal Reality is still a projection of our Personal Reality.

Shared Reality is the overlap of your Personal Reality and my Personal Reality. Our shared reality enforces the idea of a collective reality.

Collective Reality is a source of knowledge and experience built on generations of Shared Realities. It is a combination of our imagination, biology, and our experience of all things physical. We perceive it to exist independently of our own Personal Reality. We feel connected to this Collective Reality as a universal experience that has existed before we were born and will continue when we are gone. We assume all life forms to be a part of it whether we observe their experience or not. We are contributors to the Collective Reality during our lifetime.

This perspective has shaped my thoughts on the reality I experience. Most importantly, it has made me feel much more connected to what I experience as reality and has given me a greater awareness that I am the explorer charting my adventure.

Despite my own unique experience of reality (Personal Reality), I feel connected to my environment and the people in it, a sort of oneness with others within the overall experience of reality. So beyond our personal experience, there is clearly something else we are connected to (Collective Reality) in order to all relate to the experience we call life. Collective Reality, along with our Personal Reality, is in turn affected by the people we interact with (Shared Reality).

Previously, I often felt a disconnect to the power of the present moment. Lost in my thoughts of past and future. I am certainly not alone in having experienced this feeling. It is as though we are often trying to unravel our pasts and see into our futures so we can feel good about the present moment, as though how we feel currently is not something we control, that the past has happened "to" us and the future will hopefully bring better luck. As I spent time pondering my individual reality, I became more aware that I am always the interpreter of it. I began to understand that I was projecting my own Personal Reality onto everything — my own experiences as well as what I perceived as other people's reality.

Coming to terms with the fact that all I ever experience is my Personal Reality, that my Personal Reality is always being interpreted by me, I decided to see if I could change what I had once felt to be outside of my control. I started to look in the mirror and see what I wanted to see. I began to assess my personal situation and decide that if I really did have a choice, was I doing what I really wanted? Thinking about my mortality and what mattered most about being alive gave me added incentive to really consider my part in life's experience. I began to feel a deeper connection to the present moment and to experience "the now" as what we have to enjoy.

Recognizing that life isn't happening to me and that my perspective, my Personal Reality, is guided by my thoughts, creates incredible power because I can choose how I live my life. I am aware that I have a choice. It's a new perspective on what was in front of me all along, a new lens through which to see things.

We are the interpreters of our Personal Reality. How we interpret any given thing is a matter of perspective.

1. PERSONAL REALITY

To sum up, there is only one perspective on reality we experience — our own.

We are the navigators of our Personal Reality. We have a say in the experience. When presented with a choice, we choose to turn left or right, say yes or no, follow the other fish or swim off on our own. And there are always options available; it's just a matter of perspective.

Our thoughts and ideas come and go, generally out of our control, yet it is we who choose on which to take action. We are the ones who give energy to the thoughts that appear out of nowhere, and who experience the physical reactions to those thoughts. Bruce Davis, an American author who leads retreats around the world, breaks down a figure that is often quoted on the web, saying if we have "50,000 – 70,000 thoughts per day, this means between 35 and 48 thoughts per minute per person. The steady flow of thinking is a thick filter between our thoughts and feelings, our head and heart."

We write the script and we watch the movie.

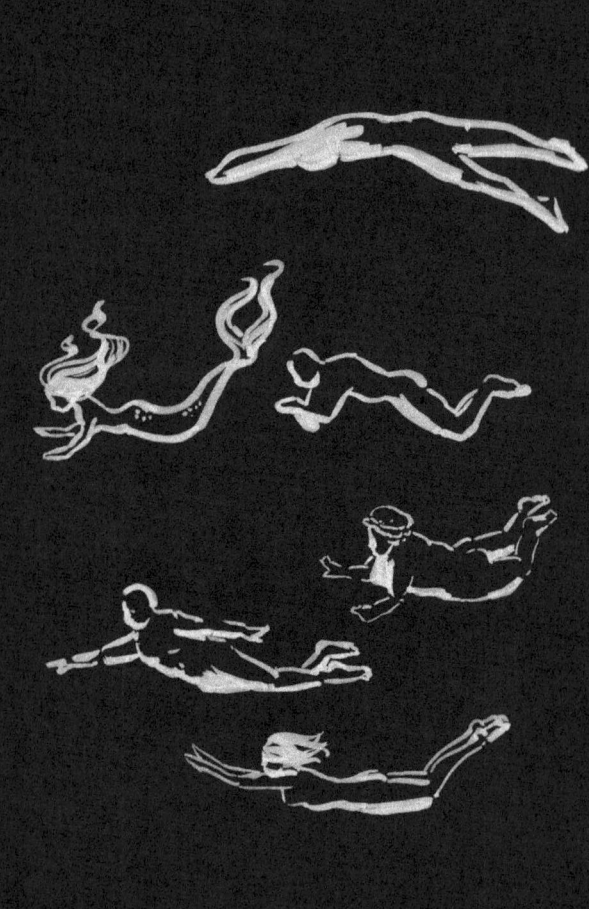

It is as though we are swimming in the Collective Reality in schools of fish, breathing our own air yet following the fish that are immediately around us (Shared Reality). The places you go, the things you see and the thoughts and feelings you have all shape your view of the world, and because you are part of a school, your experiences are reinforced by the others around you. But as in a school of fish, your experience will vary based on the type of fish you are surrounded by and the ocean you swim in. And like fish that are unaware they are swimming in water, too often we are oblivious of our own immersion in the reality we take for granted.

It is my understanding that no matter what others see, an anorexic person can see themselves as overweight in the mirror just as an overweight person can see themselves as slimmer on a day they have worked out and followed a healthy diet. How we feel in the moment affects our experience of reality. The only image that truly matters and we take seriously is the one we have of ourselves. We project the image of ourselves and then react accordingly.

Likewise, when somebody uses words to tell us how they feel or to describe something, we tend to relate to the personal experiences we connect with those particular words — we use their word choices to project our own reality into their experience.

When we jump to conclusions, whether positive or negative, about another person's actions, we are projecting our thoughts, our own reality.

> **ACTION:** *If we see our life only from the perspective of our Personal Reality, then why not be open to the idea of changing our perspective and choosing how we want to experience it? Next time you find yourself starting to project what you believe someone else feels about you, try to choose a perspective you want, because I now feel, at the end of the day, it is all in my mind.*

> **ACTION:** *To go to an extreme, who is to say anything or anyone else exists? It could all be a product of our imagination. So if you take that radical perspective for a moment, use it to envision your Personal Reality precisely as you want it to be — one small aspect at a time.*
>
> *It is entirely possible we have that amount of control.*

2. SHARED REALITY

Shared Reality — the overlap of your Personal Reality with my Personal Reality — is the most influential outside factor contributing to our Personal Reality. Our Personal Reality is shaped by the interconnected relationships we have within the networks of people we create and the information we choose to digest. These connections include friends, family and our local community, and extend to the communities we visit and with which we have a personal connection. Social media and other information we choose to consume affect our thoughts and experience of Personal Reality.

On a micro scale, Shared Reality is the overlap between people. On a much larger scale, it is the overlap that happens between generations.

Shared Reality directly impacts our Personal Reality as it affects how we perceive the world. Think how often we take at face value the things we hear from the people around us and in our networks. And we don't always make a habit of questioning the information passed on to us, yet it is influencing our thoughts and the choices we make. Our constant decision-making on small and large scales is creating our present while building our future.

If you have grown up in a household of drama, then drama is likely to become part of your Personal Reality. If you are part of a community that frowns upon nude sunbathing, then the idea of lying naked on a beach in Spain may feel uncomfortable. The Shared

Shared Reality is a significant contributor to the limitations and constraints that we apply to our lives & personal growth. It can also be the most significant contributor to positive change. You really are the people you know & the company you keep.

Reality you have with the people around you directly affects how you think and the Personal Reality you experience. It can shape the decisions you make and the trails you blaze (or don't).

The Shared Reality with the people in your social media networks can profoundly affect both your Personal Reality and your perception of the Collective Reality. Gaining knowledge through Shared Reality doesn't make the information true, but can make it appear to be true; once it resonates with you, it feels true to you too. That is the herd mentality. Now the perspective of the Shared Reality is part of your Personal Reality. Social media is exceptionally impactful as our networks are populated with peers projecting their Personal Realities as accepted truths. We tend to be a part of networks of people who have similar beliefs; it's a vicious cycle because that can mean we don't get access to unbiased and balanced information. Perspective is everything, and everything can be viewed from a different perspective.

It is worth considering that we are often not the same in private as we are in public. Our lives appear better online. With cell phones able to take high-res photos, with colour-enhancing filters and with time to select the perfect shot from a large amount of digitally taken photos, people see only what we want to share with them. What is shared can be an enhanced reality. We pick and choose small slices of our lives to share with our networks. Wanting to show the positive moments, the best hair days, the most incredible meals, the most fabulous views, and happiest smiles.

But seeing only the augmented version of people's lives, the most celebrated takes, can be very misleading. Wanting to live up to others' "enhanced reality" is tough. In contrast, there are people too who only share the negative aspects of their lives. Either end of the spectrum creates misleading insights into what appears to be the norm. This is all part of the Shared Reality that is shaping our Personal Realities (except for those who are fully unplugged, no doubt).

Sarah: *"I just read it's going to rain tomorrow!"*
Jana: *"Hey Helen, it's going to be a storm tomorrow!"*
Helen: *"I'm posting it online! 'Intense storm expected!'"*

Another aspect of our Shared Reality these days is the way that mental health is being discussed in public. Unlike, say, a broken leg, problems with mental health were often brushed aside and left to the individual person or family to deal with (or not) in private. With mental health becoming a more common subject for discussion in many countries, and with comparatively more resources available in some parts of the world, a lot more people are openly dealing with their illnesses. Social media has played a large role in bringing many more topics, including mental health, into open discussions. This sort of openness allows us to see more of the reality people are living. It's a good reminder that what we see of someone on the surface is not the whole picture.

For the most part, people only share what they want us to see. Comparing our Personal Reality to that of the perceived reality of others is difficult. Just as we need positive role models, we need a holistic view of the positive and negative elements that make up their Personal Realities. Struggle and suffering are a natural part of everyone's lives. (For the highest achievers, it can be the super fuel to persevere.)

Still, for us to feel deeply impacted in our Personal Reality by someone else's struggle or by an event, it almost always needs to have occurred in our Shared Reality. Consider how you feel when you get tragic news of somebody in your Shared Reality versus a news flash about something happening in a remote part of the world, far outside your Shared Reality. It does not impact how you feel in the same way. Positive news works the same way.

The Shared Reality you have with others affects both your Personal Reality and theirs.

ACTION: *Try putting out the kind of energy you want; you will probably get more of the same in return. Great energy inspires others and attracts like-minded people. Consider how Terry Fox inspired annual events for cancer research by running across the country to draw attention to the need for funding. When your Personal Reality brings value to others, you attract more of what you put out. This is how energy can be self-fuelling. Lead by example.*

ACTION: *If you want to be successful, surround yourself with people who embody your idea of success; enjoy life more by being around people who are enjoying life; improve your own fitness by surrounding yourself with people who are fit; see the world in a positive light surrounded by people who already see it positively; impact the world positively by surrounding yourself with people already doing it. In your reading, include books by people you aspire to be more like and pay attention to their words; choose information sources that contribute to the life you want to live, not information and people who don't. Find reasons why anything is possible rather than why everything is a struggle.*

3. COLLECTIVE REALITY

Collective Reality has three components:

a physical matter
b generational knowledge, and
c our imagination.

We can't walk through a brick wall, so in that regard, the Collective Reality we engage with is very real, with real consequences. We also know not to try to walk through a brick wall as the knowledge is passed on to us without us needing to try for ourselves. And then there are the walls that divide nations — with few exceptions (like the old Berlin Wall), those walls are purely our imagination at work.

We have constructed a concept of community and culture that is a fiction of our imagination. In this regard, Collective Reality is created by our beliefs. The things people live by — including culture, class,

Gaining knowledge through Shared Reality doesn't make the information true, but can make it appear to be true; once it resonates with you, it feels true to you too. That is the herd mentality.

nationality, companies, rules, wealth, religion and the passing of time — are seldom a part of our biology (love may be an exception), but instead are a creation of our mind and accepted by the many. It merely requires enough people to believe in them to establish them as real. Our Shared Reality enforces this Collective Reality as it requires having more than one person believe in the Collective Reality for it to exist. Having a feeling of belonging and common beliefs in a nation of people, most of whom you don't know, requires that our Shared Reality give value and power to this belief.

Our experience of the Collective Reality today is undoubtedly different from the Collective Reality future generations will experience and from the realities experienced by those who came before us. It is a cumulative experience built upon over centuries. More knowledge will be passed on, and some will get left behind. It is the foundation our current experience rests upon and is something we cannot detach ourselves from. We are born into an established Collective Reality. Someone already learned to make fire, so we don't have to. Others have already created our language, so we don't have to. Dogs are already humans' best friends, the world map and country borders established, theories of the universe and the charting of stars already available as the basis of modern science. The Collective Reality we experience is built on the knowledge of past generations' experiences coupled with the addition of our own experiences. The lessons from our experience are passed on to the next generation. What we do in our lifetime directly impacts friends, family and the people in our Shared Reality, and on a larger scale, social influencers make an even broader impact.

"I'm American. I'm Canadian." Spot the difference.

Because the Collective Reality is added to by each successive generation, what we consider to be knowledge, truth, culture, society is usually deeply ingrained into our assumptions about life.

To change the Collective Reality is almost a non-starter. That said, recognizing how these three realities intercept allows us the freedom to act as individuals and change our Personal Reality in ways that create more meaning in our lives, independent of the Collective Reality.

I believe that acknowledging the overlapping of these three realities can help us gain new perspectives and help us make decisions that positively affect our Personal Realities and that of future generations. We can do great things with new perspectives. The rules by which we abide are inventions of the culture and communities we are born into. Most of us believe in these rules enough that we have incorporated them into our own understanding of what is real in life. They are woven into the biology of the living. Our perception of the world is affected by our cultural beliefs. So breaking the rules and challenging the status quo is a significant part of how followers become leaders. It is how we create culture.

> **ACTION:** *When you next have a decision to make, consider which "facts" you are weighing as deciding factors. Are they a part of our undeniable physical, biological world, or unquestioned generational knowledge, or simply plucked out from the imagination?*

> **ACTION:** *Try to think of one long-accepted rule from the Collective Reality that you could — or would like to — break. A great place to start is by considering rules and ideas passed on to you and are not grounded in first-hand experience. During a recent conversation, a friend in the music business told me musician friends had warned him "you*

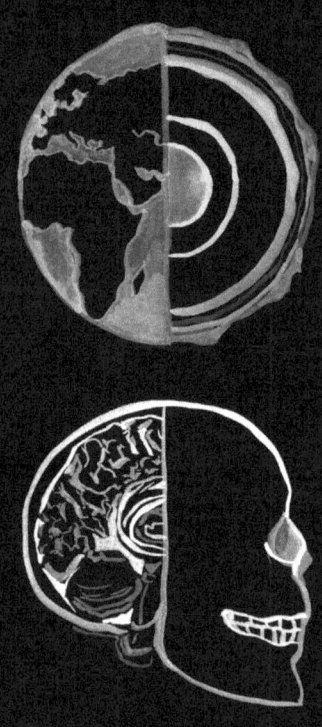

We live at the surface of a much deeper core.

can't call a record label, and you certainly can't just walk into their office, you just don't do that." He thought, "Why not? It is just a building separating me from other humans." Who says there are any established rules on how to conduct business with people in music, or any other area, that can't be broken? My friend went on to be vastly more successful than any of his peers as he chose to question the Collective Reality. Generally when somebody sets out to break a record they are faced with the opinion that it is not possible. It takes one record breaker to set the stage for the next.

As a contributor to the Collective Reality, you can ask yourself how much of the knowledge we obtain is real, and how much is just false information that has been continually passed on as real. What's your contribution?

ACTION: *Consider that our experience of the passing of time differs from that of other species. Those that are lighter with faster metabolisms to us their world seems fast-motion, to them our world must seem slow-motion. Think of the fly that gets away from the swatter with ease. The lifespan of a mayfly is a day, that is their entire lifetime! In fact some only live a number of hours. If redwood trees experience time, surely our lives must seem short. The point is that we overlap with other living creatures in a physical world yet experience a different reality. Time also feels like it passes faster when we engage in activities that are not new to us and do not require the same amount of our attention as an activity we do for the first time. As an action, sign up for an activity that is completely new. Turn off your electronic devices and show up ready to give your full attention. At the end of the day consider if the day felt longer and fuller than your average day. Pay more attention to the moment and contemplate whether your day felt longer. View the world with the idea that for some species, today is an entire lifetime.*

"A little more to the left...."

DOES CONSCIOUSNESS CREATE THE UNIVERSE?

We live in a universe perfectly formed for life. Many questions would be answered if, in fact, life were the creator of the universe. On a micro scale, we are continually creating our individual life experience with our personal choices and projections of the future. The opportunities we perceive come from our ability to find perspectives that allow us to see we have choices. Perspective is formulated in the mind. What if, on a larger scale, over time we have been creating our idea of the world around us? What if we are building what we experience, each generation adding little bits to the puzzle left behind from the last generation. Consider for example that mysterious Dark Matter in the universe might turn out to be less of a mystery in the future. As we create reality, the Collective Reality establishes it as factual for future generations.

The thought that tomorrow exists is instilled in us by the Collective Reality. I am sure that at some point in time nobody knew what would happen once the sun went down. It must have taken a while to build up the expectation of a "new day" as a dependable part of life. These ideas, which are now expectations, have all been

building up in the Collective Reality into what is now possibly a much more complex world and life experience. These expectations come pre-loaded with our "factory settings" at birth. We have rules we follow built on other people's experience. We have ideas based on generations of knowledge, and the ingrained habit of trying to prove our thoughts to be right. It is our nature to look for answers confirming our beliefs. Our Shared Realities generally challenge fresh ideas. Consequently, aha moments are in fact new thoughts, and aha moments can be few and far between.

Our minds create our world, so changing your thoughts does change your life. A new perspective can offer an entirely new experience.

In my Personal Reality, my consciousness feels infinite and ageless. I am not limited to my body nor isolated from the world outside. It is as if there is a seamlessness between myself and everything else, a sense of infinity and at-oneness with everything surrounding me. This would make sense if, in fact, everything around me is a projection of myself.

If I were inside a submarine, I would not feel the water in which I was immersed; I would be separated from my environment, yet "inside" my body and mind I feel everything. I am not disconnected from my environment. I am submerged in it, at one with it. In this way, I feel directly connected to what and how I experience.

I can't recall the feeling I have of self ever being different, no matter how my body has changed. I am no more or less myself as I age. I have been myself for

as long as I can remember. I am not my body, and I am not my thoughts. I am the quiet observer of the movie of my life.

Ah yes, life was so much easier back then...

I am intrigued by the writing of the American scientist Robert Lanza, MD and his Theory of Biocentrism — the concept that the universe does not create consciousness but that instead, consciousness creates the universe. In other words, the entire universe is in our minds. If you choose to believe this perspective, then the idea of Personal Reality is more relevant than ever.

Is he going up or going down?

PUTTING IT INTO PERSPECTIVE

I work with a lot of clients as a consultant — at least, that's how the relationship starts. It quite often turns into life coaching, the reason being that I believe the answers to a lot of the bigger-picture questions clients have, especially those who help people take their next step, are already available to them — they just need a new perspective. Helping people tap into their creativity and internal knowledge through life coaching and personal development can lead to both finding answers and asking the right questions.

Perspective is everything; the ability to gain a new perspective on any situation is invaluable. There is always a better lens you can be looking through. The key is to recognize we can change the lens at will.

When the idea of three overlapping realities struck me, it clicked for me as a new perspective that could be helpful in seeing the bigger picture. What you feel, what you experience and what you believe are always your Personal Reality; acknowledging that in itself should already help you see that your view on life can be changed and that consequently your feelings, experiences and beliefs could change too. Taking a

"Try on these glasses, you may prefer what you see...."

new perspective on your internal thoughts impacts your perspective on everything external in your life.

At a distance we are seen as one.

ALONE TOGETHER

Suggesting that we experience only our own Personal Reality is not the same as saying we should be egotistical and self-centred. We are part of a bigger whole; we are waves in the ocean. It is not about taking selfish actions or suggesting that only our individual selves matter — we are interconnected. I am merely offering a perspective to contemplate. Beyond empathy, we are not really able to experience reality through others; we each have only our own Personal Reality. Becoming aware that our thoughts judge our external experiences as either positive or negative and our minds interpret our thoughts allows us to consider how we choose to respond to situations. It is how we can turn something "negative" into a positive experience. If we can take more control of our actions because we are aware we have a choice, we can lead happier lives. Improving our Personal Reality improves our Shared Reality, and ultimately impacts the Collective Reality. It could be a part of how we can have an impact on how we achieve greater peace and harmony in the world.

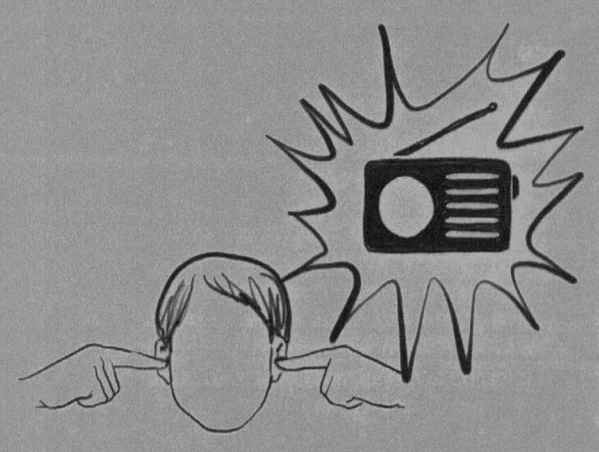

If you don't like what's playing, turn it off.

WHAT IS, IS AND WHAT WILL BE, IS NOT

What is, is. Your current circumstances are what you perceive them to be. If you have broken your leg, no amount of thoughts will fix it miraculously. In fact, no amount of positive or negative thoughts will change what already is. If you suffered significant trauma at some point in your life, the past does not get erased. If you have been addicted, something drove you to addiction. Before moving past a circumstance, you first have to acknowledge without judgment that it has happened or still exists. You can want your situation to be different, but you cannot change what already is. What you can do is move on from the past and immediately start to make a change in the present. Accepting what is allows you to deal with it directly and decide what comes next. It's like saying you don't like the music that's playing. First, you have to acknowledge that it is playing and then you need to decide if you will turn it off. However, spending time complaining about the music is not going to change the present or future. Chances are you will still be listening to the music you don't like.

Acknowledge the elephant in the room, then ask it to leave.

"Does anyone mind if I ask it to leave?"

The problem arising when we consider ourselves to be the interpreters of our thoughts, the creators of our Personal Reality, is that we can feel resentment toward ourselves at the notion we *create our own suffering*. Our lives up to this point are an accumulation of experiences that for better or worse have made us the individuals we are today. How you react at any given moment to the "now" is always justifiable to yourself. Accept your actions and judgments from the past were justifiable at the time and now they reside in the past. There is usually a period of time, even after we recognize our bad habits and negative patterns, when we continue to make the same mistakes while we figure out how to change.

We are always doing the best we can with what we've got, no matter what it looks like to other people. Michael Neil, who is both an internationally renowned transformative coach and a bestselling author, puts it this way: "We do what we do because it seems like a good idea at the time in our thought-created inner world." That really sums up the universal cause of all human behaviour.

You are exactly where you are supposed to be — that, it turns out, is a well-known saying, but it really made an impact the first time I heard it, when a friend was speaking to me. To that I would add: You will always be exactly where you are meant to be. If you feel in any way responsible for your past suffering, consider you have reached a new level of possibilities as you now feel empowered by what you can do with your present moment. You just had to get here. We are continually evolving and should never judge ourselves for our past. You can have been beaten down and have the scars to show; it's getting back up that is essential. It is equally as important not to carry the baggage forward. What matters now is to recognize the choice we have in how to interpret our thoughts and our ability to seize opportunities. What will be has not yet materialized.

> **ACTION**: *Observe your past and recognize that your decisions, circumstances and network, among other things, have played a role for better or worse in getting you to exactly where you are. Acknowledge what you would like to change and confront it by first accepting its existence; then recognizing in life the one constant is change, and establish steps to take moving forward so you will be exactly where you are supposed to be.*

Young man: *"I'm sinking!"*
Blind man: *"Vat are you sinking about?"*

THE POWER OF WORDS

Words are symbols with complex and multi-layered meanings. If I say "the colour blue", you may envision a particular shade of blue, the sky, the ocean, a specific car from your memory, a feeling, a sound, a smell … and for every person, the word has a slightly or drastically different significance. We may think our audience understands our words to have the exact meanings the words have for us, but in fact we have individual experiences with words and their meanings.

Our attachments to the meaning of words is part of our tendency to project our reality and assume others understand what we are expressing. Equally, people

does the language
we speak affect
our life experience?

project their choice of words. This is where misunderstandings can take place.

"I can fit 10 words into one character!"

Words can spark emotions in people resulting in inspiring performances. When someone resonates with words spoken to them, those words become part of that person's Personal Reality. When words impact a large group of people, the reaction in the Shared Reality amplifies the power of the words in each person's Personal Reality.

Imagine a trainer or coach telling a team at the most critical of times to get back out there and win, become heroes, champions, show the world what they are made of. At the moment the athletes believe they can do it, the Shared Reality powers the individual realities, potentially inspiring incredible performances. Ultimately to persuade somebody is to have that person accept into their Personal Reality the thoughts you project.

If trainers and coaches were to tell athletes they were going to lose, that they would make fools of themselves, that they would suffer great pain and embarrassment, imagine what the result would be. A great performance? I don't think so! The same applies to the Shared Reality we experience of the world through the news we choose to read, hear and watch. The people we surround ourselves with and the information we choose to ingest ultimately impact our Personal Reality and our own "performance." The Shared Reality can empower us to be the best version of ourselves and see the world in a positive light, or it can help us lose hope and sight of our dreams, or contribute to a belief that we live in a terrible world. Words matter. Who we listen to matters too.

Which voice do you listen to?

The words you select will have a different effect on different people based on their personal experiences

attached to your words of choice. Don't underestimate the power your words have on the listener. Choose your words and audience wisely.

> **ACTION**: *Find and read a short story. Ask a friend to read it too. Compare notes on how each of you imagined the characters to look and sound and on the scenery that surrounded them. Review the differences in interpretations and mental imagery that the words created for each of you. Observe that just a few words are able to generate elaborate mental imagery and emotional connection for the reader.*

> **ACTION**: *Find words in different languages that are difficult to translate into English with only one word. For example, according to the* Collins English Dictionary *the Scottish word* tartle *means "the act of hesitating while introducing someone because you have forgotten their name." I particularly like the Japanese word* komorebi, *which means the interplay of light and leaves when sunlight shines through trees, and the Hebrew word* Firgun, *which means to whole-heartedly appreciate the success of others. Do any people other than the Inuit have a noun like* iktsuarpok, *which is the feeling of anticipation while you wait for someone to arrive and that results in the urge to intermittently go outside to check for them?*

"My grandmother used to have a ring very much like the one you are wearing...."

COMMUNICATING OPENLY

Small talk and mincing our words can play a significant role in our conversations with the people we meet. In these cases we exert energy talking but with little value in what we say. This is part of the etiquette established by the Collective Reality of our culture. We need to reduce empty words and instead consciously dive into meaningful conversations. Often when a person you have just met says "It feels like I have known you forever," it is because right away you have been able to jump into an authentic conversation that resonates on a deep level. Being vulnerable in your openness creates a deeper connection and establishes trust. This, in turn, allows you to be yourself right from the start. Superficial talk is the equivalent of junk food.

"Want to talk about the weather?"
"No thanks."

ACTION: *Next time you meet someone, or you talk to someone you know superficially and would like to know better, try talking to them as though you have known them your whole life. Be vulnerable. Put yourself out there by being open with your thoughts and use personal experiences to allow others to do the same. Say more of what is on your mind, even to strangers with whom you feel a connection. If you are in the elevator with somebody you are interested in talking to, tell them you are interested in talking to them, and you can even say you are not sure what to talk about. Guaranteed, it will start a conversation that is unlikely to have the weather in the opening line. You may lose some relationships, but you will make and keep the ones that matter the most. The more you take this approach, the more incredible opportunities will arise from these deeper relationships. Your life will be filled with more meaning and your network will be stronger.*

When life gives you a giant lemon on the back of a flatbed truck...

THAT'S MY STORY, AND I'M STICKING TO IT!

Within the context of Shared Reality, the effect of influence goes both ways. Those in your Shared Reality are influencing your thoughts and decisions; however, you are also affecting their perception of you.

You are projecting your story and those who know you are solidifying it. If you are trying to change and be known for something else, if you want to be thought of as always having good luck instead of always being unlucky, you need to become aware of the story you have been projecting. It is hard to change when those around you have categorized you by your past actions. I can think of many people who always find success out of their failures and seem to be creating their own opportunities under any circumstance. There are others who almost always fail to make good on the opportunities that are handed to them. Consequently, those who always make good of a situation are more likely to be given more opportunities. It is a snowball effect.

Becoming aware of what you are putting out is extremely important. What you put out is getting fed back to you, and as you know, you are being affected by

the words and information that is spread in your Shared Reality.

Creating a vision for yourself and living up to it with your actions is critical.

"Once upon a time, there lived a very happy, healthy, successful, person named: me...."

ACTION: *Create a vision board to help you see and feel yourself developing a new story. Start putting out the image you want others to connect with you. Ask someone to describe you — how they think of you. It can help you to become aware of how people interpret your story. You would like people to share the same view of you as you have of yourself. Their perception of you can re-enforce your new self image.*

MANIFESTING YOUR PERSONAL REALITY

You need to see the top of the mountain, devise a route, know what you need to take up with you, then put your focus on the very next small step, then the next, then the next, so that when you look up again you will have almost arrived. Of course, the planning happens before you even leave your home — you need to have identified the mountain and how to get there, have a timeline to accomplish your goals, have envisioned the climb up, the safe return, the excitement of the unknown, and the openness of where it leads next. You need to envision the bigger picture, break it down into small steps, and then follow through with the plan.

When you don't take action on your ideas and instead wait for somebody to do it for you, you are waiting for them to give importance to your Personal Reality in their own. Taking action needs to matter most of all to you. You need to take the first step. Don't wait, because in your life you only have the experience of your Personal Reality and what happens is up to you, nobody else. You can either see yourself surrounded by endless opportunities to take action or

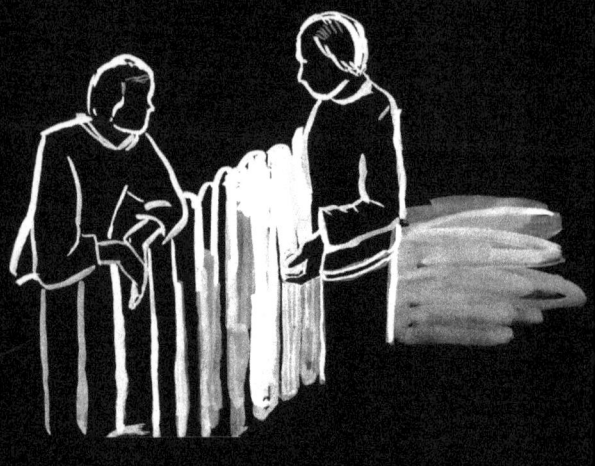

Neighbour 1: *"How's your house coming along?"*
Neighbour 2: *"Just waiting for you to build it...."*

have an excuse as to why nothing ever works out for you. The latter puts all action and results outside your control, beyond your Personal Reality.

The things you focus on naturally develop. It is how nothing becomes something. It starts with a thought and extends into a plan first, then action steps, and finally the results of the actions taken. Whatever you give energy to manifests. Every action has a reaction. How could it not? Give energy to the things you want to manifest, not the stuff you don't. You really can make a mountain out of a molehill. You are continually creating your Personal Reality first through thought and then by taking action on your thoughts. Dream it, do it. If you decide to build a house and work on it every day, there will come a day when the house is built. If you do nothing else but focus on building your house, it gets built faster than if you try and do ten other things at the same time. Not only does a home get built quicker but it gets made more thoroughly with attention to detail because you are focused on it exclusively, you are putting all your energy into achieving your goal. From finding the money to laying the first brick. When your goal is clear, your perspective on the small steps to get to it changes. Suddenly the things that might have felt unrelated to your goal have their place in achieving your vision. Once you have a "why," the "how" changes as things fall into place.

If you want to build a house, but you don't work on it, you don't give it time and energy, will it build itself? How long would it take until somebody else decides to

Connect the dots to see the happy face.

make it for you? Your Personal Reality is entirely driven by your thoughts and actions, not those of others. However, if you take action, you will naturally attract people and things that fit into the puzzle you are building. Like a jigsaw puzzle, if you know what the finished image looks like, then you more easily recognize the pieces you are looking for. The next piece can be right in front of you, but until you know you are looking for it, you won't see it. When you start taking control of your reality by designing it, you become aware of the pieces around you, the dots that are already there and just need connecting.

When you are feeling miserable, it is hard, if not impossible, to envision the reality you desire. However, when you are feeling energized, empowered and upbeat, you are much better positioned to take on the world. Time to start feeling empowered!

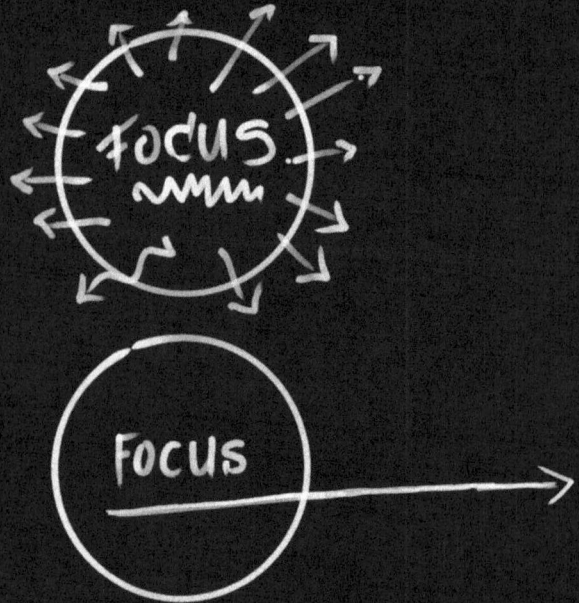

The difference between putting energy into many things versus one thing is that when you focus, you go a lot further.

ACTION: *Music and exercise often help me to get back into the right frame of mind. So combine the two. Get up, get active and get your favorite upbeat dance jams going. Work your way up over at least a couple of songs to your favourite power track. Turn up the volume loud and move your body to the beat. Jump around, sing along, until you are smiling and feeling good. Something else might occur to you in the moment — going for a walk, talking with a friend, whatever your inner wisdom suggests. Now take a moment to recognize that only your perspective on your current state of mind has changed. It is an internal shift in perspective. This change in attitude to the situation is a micro step in your timeline yet a macro step in altering your perspective of your Personal Reality. Consider that at the core of happiness, success, meaning, fulfillment, well-being, contentment and a sense of purpose is a shift in your internal perspective of your Personal Reality. Your moment of euphoria when combining aerobic exercise with upbeat and uplifting music is a small sample of changing your experience by changing your perspective.*

LEAVING YOUR COMFORT ZONE

I remember standing at a dock. Every day I would watch as somebody else jumped in while I stood still, concerned it would be too cold. After a few days, I lowered my body into the water. It was cold, but soon enough I didn't want to get out. The next day I jumped in without waiting. The impact of the cold was less, and I adjusted to the temperature much faster than the day before. I didn't want to get out. The water was beautiful. The following day I took a run and jumped out as far as I could. The water caught me, and I adjusted to the temperature almost immediately. Why didn't I do this the first day? So often we fear the unknown. We are afraid of the impact. Once you realize how quickly you will adapt, it becomes a question of just how far you are willing to throw yourself into the unknown.

When you throw yourself into the unknown, the feeling of commitment to the action is visceral. It's what wholehearted commitment feels like. It's the feeling you get when your feet have left the dock and your body has not yet hit the water, yet your mind has already accepted the impact. In my Personal Reality, the water is always there to catch me. I live with the

Life BEGINS at the end of your Comfort zone

idea that life begins at the end of my comfort zone and I will always adapt. Taking action can be hard and uncomfortable if you don't trust you can always adjust. Manifesting something you don't currently have will only come through taking new actions.

ACTION: *Assess your current level of comfort in a regular activity. Become aware of when you are holding yourself back from doing something out of your ordinary due to overthinking and not taking action right away. Next time you reach the end of your comfort zone, take one more step!*

TAKING ACTION

When something inspires you to take action, take action right away. Go with the feeling of excitement that rises from within you. (Of course, it goes without saying that I am encouraging positive and ethical actions. Now is never the time to become a criminal!) Results come from actions. Big actions have big results. Big results come faster when action is taken right away. The time is now. In fact, it just passed by. That's how fast the right moment can pass. So when you feel your gut telling you to do something, take action right away. Once the idea goes from your stomach to your head, your analytical mind kicks in and starts coming up with reasons not to take action.

I used to take people cliff jumping into the water, and there was one particular jump that required a difficult climb up. Once you got to the ledge, it was complicated to climb back down. Jumping was your best option. Most people would reach the ledge and jump right away. They had committed to the jump before they even climbed up to the ledge. Others, however, would stand on the ledge looking down at the water below, and if more than five seconds passed, they would become paralyzed, unable to jump.

"Ready or not, here I come!"

Suddenly the determined thrill seekers were concerned individuals questioning their commitment to taking a leap of faith. If you wait and overthink through your initial gut feeling, what could have been an incredible experience becomes an opportunity lost. The longer you dwell on it, the less likely you are to take action. Nike got it right: "Just Do It." Yoda got it right: "Do. Or do not. There is no try."

Experience a leap of faith.

Commit to the process and detach from the outcome. That doesn't mean keeping your eyes off the prize, it just means if you don't focus on the action leading towards your desired outcome, you won't reach it. Being present in the here and now and stopping your thoughts of past and future allows you to give your highest performance. So take action with the focus on the process and not the outcome.

> **ACTION**: *Write a list of the five smallest steps you can take today to get closer to the biggest goals you have set. Do this each day. Focus on taking action on each one of these steps without daydreaming about the end destination. Be present and enjoy the journey.*

METAMORPHOSIS

At some point in your life, you go from depending on others to depending on yourself. This personal change happens at different times for different people. Some of us have no choice but to grow up faster than others. In the cycle of family, there is a clearly defined moment when you go from being the child to becoming the parent. During the time you are dependent on others, it is hard to feel that you have the ability to materialize your future as you want it. It is easier to look for help and guidance than to look within and help yourself. During that period, you are also a significant part of your caregivers' Personal Reality. You are a driving force for them to provide what you need. But as time goes on, you need to be able to provide for yourself, and then for others. And it is in that transition more than ever that you need to become aware and acknowledge that your thoughts and actions are forming your Personal Reality.

    What I feel is directly connected to what I think. Take fear for example. Fear in my opinion exists only in response to some thought about the future. Even when you stand on the edge of a cliff and look down, the sensation you are having is the reaction to the

"Nooooo....Nooooo...Nooooo!!!"

thought of falling. You have not yet fallen. The action you are afraid of has not yet happened, however you are reacting to it as though it is real now. When you take a step back from your thoughts and recognize that your current state of mind and your physical sensations of well-being are connected to your thoughts, you can become more selective about the thoughts you empower and the ones you don't.

We do not have to dwell or react to every thought we have. We spend too much time worrying in the present moment about something that has not yet happened. Not only do we cease to enjoy the moment, but we become blind to the things that are available to us in the here and now which can positively affect our future. In one of the Austin Powers movies, there is a scene in which a man is going to get run over by a steamroller. He is standing in its path a considerable distance away. The steamroller is moving at a snail's pace, toward the victim who is neither tied up nor otherwise physically impeded from moving out of its way. Not only that, but at the speed the steamroller is moving it will be some time before there is any impact, enough time to escape disaster and make some tea. But instead the person cries in fear, not moving and assuming their fate without attempting to change it. We do this ourselves in our day-to-day life all too often. Instead of taking action now to create the outcome we want, we assume our projected future is already a reality. Our energy then goes to bracing for the impact. We subsequently create the future we don't want by preparing for the worst.

whatever you give ENERGY to manifests

Whatever you give energy to manifests.

It works both ways: we don't want to react to a projected negative future, AND we need to create a vision of what we do want to manifest. We can have a tough time envisioning our future selves feeling different from how we feel today. We project our current state into the future. But, as the Greek philosopher Heraclitus is credited with saying, the only constant in life is change. And so we ourselves change — our physical bodies, our thoughts, our individual situations.... If you start going to the gym every day and following a healthy diet, you will not look or feel the same in the future as you do now. It's like being broke and saying how will I ever be able to buy a house or car, or travel? The fact is that you may feel a victim of your current circumstance, but you will not be in your current circumstances when you buy the house. A new financial situation will provide you the opportunity and freedom to purchase what you want. And when you get to that point, both you and your financial situation will have changed. Recognizing that you will change, you will evolve, is the first step in evolving. If you are trying to lose weight, the sooner you see yourself with a new body shape, the faster the change will happen. Remember, it is your Personal Reality... How do you want to look? How do you want to live? Can you see yourself in this new reality? If you are unable to envision your metamorphosis, then you are only projecting your current self and situation into your future. You have to believe that the evolution of your Personal Reality is your creation so you might as

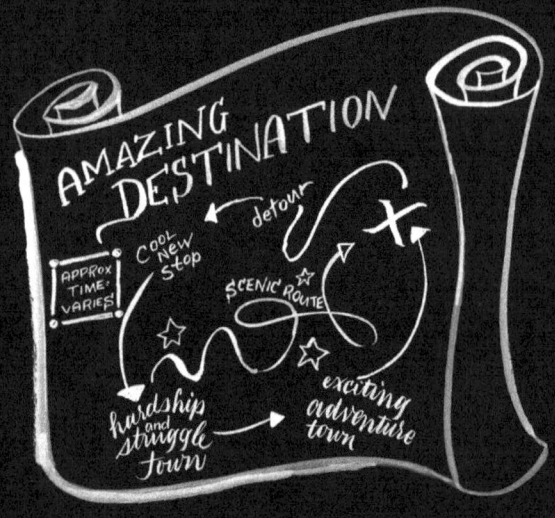

well create exactly what you want it to be. Once you envision the future you want, you can begin to identify with the person you will become. The more you feel you are the creator of your Personal Reality, the more you find that coincidences don't exist, and the more things fall into place.

"The child is father of the man." – William Wordsworth.

All this is not to say that struggles or tough times in general will be avoided; it is not to say you will find your path right away. However, you have to believe you are already on course for the destination you desire. There can be detours, flat tires and wrong turns, and also you might find you want to spend more time along the way, enjoying the journey. Being open to unexpected encounters on your journey can take you in an entirely new direction, one better than you had ever envisioned. You just needed to set yourself a course then you will find your path. During hard times you have to remind yourself you are en route to where

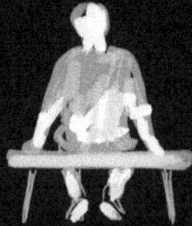

Value lies in the eye of the beholder.

you want to go; don't get caught up in the moment. It's like getting a flat tire and giving up on reaching your destination. The faster you address the issue and deal with it, the quicker you will be back on your way.

Often people get caught up in their misery and take away from the time they could be spending on addressing the problem and coming up with a solution that allows them to get to the good stuff sooner. The longer you whine about a flat tire, the longer it's going to take you to get back on the road. Pay attention to why you got the flat tire in the first place and move on with the knowledge gained. It is your Personal Reality, make it what you want it to be.

Working with a lot of creative people, especially musicians, I have found many have a hard time putting a high value on their talent and work. Often, they need external validation to feel valued, a need for others to assign their value. The problem is that you have to recognize your value first — believe in yourself for others to believe in you.

When you visit a farmers' market and see an artist selling their paintings, the art draws you in. It may be stunning work, something you would be willing to pay much more for than is marked on the price tag. However, how often do you overpay the artist for their work? Would you go out of your way to pay ten times the price tag? Now let's imagine that you have purchased the piece of art for a steal of a deal and it is hanging on your wall; what is its value to you now? Does the original price tag affect your perception of its value? Does where you purchased it change the value?

The helping
— HAND —
you are looking for
is at the end of your
— OWN —
····· — arm — ·····

From the perspective of Personal Reality, you are the one setting your work's value, and you are also affecting the demand for your work.

As you shift from being a dependant to a provider, you are able to raise your value. You are left with no other choice. I remember asking friends in the Southern States how they could afford to have eight kids and they told me, "The more kids came, the more money came." They had to provide. They had no option. Being a provider is key to acquiring what you want and indeed what you need. You automatically raise your bar. Being a provider does not require having children, it requires having a sense of the need to provide, the right frame of mind, a sense of meaning and the ability to fulfil your purpose without counting on anyone else.

If you want to have a positive impact on the world, first positively impact your own Personal Reality. Your Personal Reality affects the Shared Reality you have with others. By affecting the Shared Reality, you can influence the Collective Reality. It has to start with you. Lead by example. If you want to move people to action, it happens through Shared Reality.

ACTION: *Just like an athlete visualizing a perfect outcome at a sports event or a musician visualizing themselves playing effortlessly in front of a large audience, visualize the immediate future you want to manifest, unfolding — envision it to be easily obtainable and see yourself already enjoying it. The action of visualization is like rehearsing; the more you know your part, the better you play it on the day of the event. Envisioning yourself in the future is as real as remembering yourself in the past.*

ACTION: *Don't dwell on negative moments. Work to reduce the amount of time dwelling on what has already happened and instead see how quickly you can start working on the solution. Catch yourself when you become aware that you are dragging out what is already done and in the past. Failing teaches us more than succeeding. If you are feeling down because of a failure, consider that the lesson learned will allow you to move forward with more experience and the ability to succeed where you once failed.*

ACTION: *Write a high number representing the monetary value of your time/talent/work you would feel uncomfortable asking another person to pay you. Next write a lower number that you would feel very comfortable asking to be paid. Without sharing the numbers you wrote, ask a friend to do the same. Notice how much higher or lower their numbers are than yours. Your comfort level for asking is entirely personal and is created by you. It likely varies greatly according to what you are asking for — money versus almost anything else (a glass of water, jumper cables for your car, the time, a ride, a place to sleep, a meal ...). With this in mind, identify what the worst is that could happen if you ask above your comfort zone. In fact I will tell you what it is: the person you are asking might say no. By raising your own bar you automatically raise your own value.*

FRUSTRATION

It can be hard to keep up with our ambition and the vision we have created for ourselves. Not reaching milestones in the time frames we have set can be frustrating. The tendency is to shoot for the moon and to feel frustrated when we land among the stars because we feel we've missed our target. On these occasions, we need to review how far we have come, not how far there is left to go. Consider your past and present successes, big and small. Have you been in this place before? Did it permanently stop you from continuing your journey? (Of course, it didn't).

If you consider the worst things you have experienced, they have not stopped you from having your best experiences too. It is just time separating those experiences from one another. So accept your frustration has a time limit and it is just a bump in the road you are on. Let the feeling be, don't aggravate it more. It will pass faster if you don't add more logs to its fire.

<—————|—|—————>

before

after

FRUSTRATION

ACTION: *Review the moments in the past that led up to your most significant accomplishments. What were the circumstances permitting you to rise to the occasion? After a period of frustration did you then experience motivation? Recognizing progress in your journey so far is key to staying on your path, even if the road appears to be uphill at times.*

ACTION: *What is the cause of your frustration? Identify what level of reality it is coming from: Personal, Shared, or Collective Reality. It is always experienced in your Personal Reality, but it can be rooted in Shared Reality or Collective Reality. Recognize the root of your frustration, then let it go.*

JUDGMENT

The Collective Reality has moulded us to fit into society and its idea of success and happiness. As a result, we strive for standards sometimes impossible to attain. When we fall short, we can be incredibly hard on ourselves and judge ourselves as failures. To make things tougher, the Collective Reality is starting to promote the idea that we should always be "happy," be eternal optimists. Feeling down or having a bad day is sometimes portrayed as unacceptable. As a result, we are tough on ourselves when we are unable to be positive all the time. The cycle is vicious.

From the time we start to learn language, the voice in our head begins to have a say in how we feel. It tells us we are a failure when we don't achieve the goals we set. We are critical of ourselves when we don't live up to these expectations. Not only are we each the judge of ourselves but it seems rare not to have other people's interests in mind or at least opinions when we make decisions too. It can feel like they also are judging our actions. The problem with worrying about what other people think and what we believe is expected is that we start to distance ourselves from our own opinion, we begin to doubt our actions.

When considering our Personal Reality, we need to remind ourselves that our experience is led by our decisions. If we want to live our way, we need to make choices that do not require permission from others.

A friend once shared with me what he calls "the friend's hot shower process" and it is how he sees the acceptance of innovative ideas. When taking a shower at a new place for the first time you might find yourself endlessly trying to turn up the hot water while the water continues to be cold. At some point the water suddenly becomes too hot and you might even burn yourself and jump out. This is what happens with innovative and new ideas. At first those around you don't get it. And it may take a while for anyone to get it. But when they do everyone suddenly adopts it as their own. You see this all the time with new trends. Or a song you don't like and then you do. So when you want to make a decision that can truly change your life, keep in mind it is normal that those around you might question it, or that you may question it yourself, but remember that in order to experience something new you need to take a new action. New takes a while to feel normal.

ACTION: *Practice paying less attention to the voice in your head, especially when it makes you self-doubt. See your inner voice as an opinion, another option, but one you don't have to act on. It too only has past experiences to reference. Take in what others have to say and also realize it is just their opinion based on their Personal Reality. Make the decision you want, and accept that the outcome may not be approved by everyone. At least not right away. Taking action in the present can make for acceptance of your action in the future. Just like everything else in life, the opinions of others can change.*

Boy: "Want to go to the beach?"
Girl: "Not right now, I want to drag out feeling angry for a little bit longer. Thanks for the invitation though!"

ANGER & BLAME

Frustration can quickly escalate to anger, especially if we externalize the reasons for our emotional state. Blaming others for the situation is a way to escape ownership of our emotions. No matter what leads you to experience anger, you always need to take ownership of how you feel. You may have a good reason to feel the way you do, but letting anger take over and blaming others for it is letting go of your own responsibility for how you feel.

Blame carries forward a past action instead of confronting the problem and coming up with a solution.

Blaming others slows us down in taking positive actions to change our situation. The longer we spend feeling anger, the harder it is to feel empowered and in control of our emotions. It is a cycle that can only be broken by our change in perspective within our Personal Reality.

Being compassionate with yourself and others will bring you well-being and greater joy in life. It will help you to recognize the suffering of others, and to see yourself in them.

> **ACTION:** *Next time you feel angry, put your current state into perspective: imagine being far in the future, looking back at this moment, and ask yourself whether you would still feel the need for such anger.*

> **ACTION:** *Turn to the next section of this book to learn basic breathing techniques and mindfulness, which will help you distance yourself from the kind of thoughts that lead you to feel angry. Consequently, you can create new neural pathways enabling you to react in more compassionate ways to situations which in the past have resulted in the feeling of anger.*

Observing the cascading waterfall of thoughts. Watching the torrent without getting wet.

MINDFULNESS

I'm one of those who feel that when our experience of life first begins — at birth or perhaps even earlier — our natural state is that of balance and alignment of mind, body, and spirit. We start with well-being as a factory setting. However, as we develop language and gain the experiences of the Collective Reality and our Shared Reality, our monkey mind begins to overwhelm our inner space with thoughts. As we react to our thoughts and judge our resulting actions, we get out of alignment and become imbalanced. The imbalance affects our mood, habits, decision-making, actions and overall well-being.

As we suffer from internal imbalance, a big part of the Collective Reality suggests we should look to external stimulation to fix how we feel on the inside. This becomes a vicious cycle as we distance ourselves further and further from mind, body and spirit alignment. The important consideration is that we are naturally balanced, and we need to stop the negative cycle at the thought level.

In the words of American mindfulness teacher Jon Kabat-Zinn, mindfulness is "paying attention in a

You are only
one thought
away from
HAPPINESS

particular way: on purpose, in the present moment, and non-judgmentally."

Practising mindfulness helps you step back from your thoughts. It allows you to become aware that you are the quiet observer of your thoughts. As if watching clouds in a sky gently pass by, you see your thoughts for what they are and can act accordingly. As you learn to quieten your mind, you come to realize that we generally walk around greatly detached from the present moment as our minds are clouded with thoughts that distract us from experiencing the now. These thoughts may be about the past or the future, creating depression or anxiety. As we engage with our thoughts, we can create challenges for ourselves. Acting on negative thoughts creates challenges resulting in more negative thinking and the feeling we call "stress." We need to step back from our thinking, and consider which thoughts to act on.

I grew up believing our thoughts create our future. Now I believe our thoughts also create our present. Our thoughts are responsible for how we as individuals feel right now. It is through practicing mindfulness and becoming aware of the transient nature of our thoughts that we become more mindful of our reactions and behaviour. We can be selective in the attention we pay to our thoughts, with which ones to engage with and which ones to let pass.

To make decisions and have a clear vision, to know what we are passionate about and what our purpose is, we need to have a clear mind. Always thinking and engaging with our thoughts, especially reacting to

Young man: *"Time flies when you're having fun."*
Monk: *"Time slows down when you're in the now."*
And both are true, only time is not.

them physically, takes us further away from clarity in our vision. Our Personal Reality is made up of our thoughts and how we act on them. The vision we have of ourselves needs to come from clarity. Meditation can help us find that clarity and provide us with meaningful answers sometimes obscured by our monkey mind. It enables us to choose wisely where we set our attention and intention.

> **ACTION:** *To get started with mindfulness meditation, leave behind any preconceptions or prejudices that you may have about meditation. Find a place to sit quietly. Sit upright with your spine engaged. You have the option of letting your tongue lie flat in your mouth and allowing your neck muscles to relax, or resting the tip of your tongue against the inside of your upper front teeth — some say that stops the organ of speech in its tracks. Close your eyes and follow your breath; this will help ground you in the here and now. Breathe in, pause, and breathe out. It is in the pause in between where we are indeed just "being" and not "doing." Start to recognize when your mind wanders and gently bring it back to your breath. You will quickly find how often you are distracted by thoughts. They appear so seamlessly that it might take you a few seconds or even longer to realize you have drifted off into those thoughts. You will notice how many different thoughts come almost at once. Complete thoughts. Partial thoughts. Don't judge them, merely*

recognize them and bring your attention back to your breath. (For me personally, having a sound — something that reminds me to concentrate on my breathing — helps with focusing on the present moment. But some people don't agree with that approach because they say it means you are dictating a certain mood.) On the out breath, you may choose to gently hum to anchor yourself to the present moment with vibration. But find what works for you, a time that works for you, and a place that works for you. Whatever works, works. I find myself practising mindfulness throughout the day, when I am alone, and in the presence of others — and note that you don't need to have your eyes closed. Practising mindfulness can even help me to listen to others more deeply and stop my train of thought from interfering.

Spending some time each day practising mindful meditation and experiencing mindfulness can give us space and awaken us to the moment.

ACTION: *You may want to try this method of meditation instead. Following a friend's advice, I sometimes breathe in and say "receive" silently or "I'm breathing in, I know I'm breathing in" while making sure my belly rises with the inhale, ensuring deep and relaxing breathing. With the exhale I say "give" or "I'm breathing out, I know I'm breathing out."*

Stop thinking -about- HOW and tap into your WHY

MEANING

Feeling fulfilled in your Personal Reality is directly tied to purpose and sense of meaning. Meaning comes from within; it requires we connect to ourselves. To discover our purpose requires that we experience life. It also requires that we go deep and uncover what it is we most desire. Once we have a "why," we will encounter an endless supply of "how." It is not an external exercise.

Personal Reality is what we have. All too often Shared Reality and the Collective Reality dictate how we live our lives, what is acceptable to society, and what we believe we should do with our lives. The Shared Reality you experience could be keeping you from finding your purpose and sense of meaning. It might be stopping you from exploring a new career or getting up and performing on a stage; it might be taking your confidence away from learning a new language; it may be taking the wind from beneath your wings before you have even tried to fly. You may be passing by the one thing or person who could inspire you for the rest of your life, just because the actions you need to take are too far removed from the acceptance of the Shared Reality you are surrounded by. Because of this, you have to remind yourself that the only reality you experience, the one that matters most of all, is your own, your Personal Reality. For this reason, you need to permit yourself to follow your heart, not leave the decision-making up to the Shared Reality. If what you believe in is out of the grasp of the people who surround you, it is time to share a reality with people who inspire you to reach for the stars.

Our Shared Reality is part of our personal development; the experiences we live help us discover our passion. With passion, we pursue learning and develop more of what fulfils us. If you play an instrument, your passion will build your skills and provide you with the drive you need to grow and become more skilful. It is essential to find people and sources of information that expose us to new experiences and spark new ideas in ourselves. Some of the most celebrated stories of people that have affected the world involved those who have risen from humble beginnings and come from small towns. They broke the moulds of the limitations they grew up with and brought a new sense of opportunity to their lives by being part of new Shared Realities.

The only reality we experience is our own, so we need to be in touch with our intuition. Listening to our inner voice is essential. Our gut reaction, our intuition has profound knowledge.

People choose to work with people they trust. Trust is at the root of business itself. It is at the heart of relationships of all kinds. A person, a company, an organization that creates from a sense of meaning and authenticity is going to instil trust as they present themselves as authentic.

Lacking a sense of meaning and purpose comes with a feeling of emptiness, a lack of self-worth, a lack of drive and interest in the pursuit of goals. Many people suffer great wrongdoings, hardships and horrendous personal experiences, however when they have meaning in their lives, they can be the strongest and most successful people to walk the earth. What happens to you does not matter as much as what drives you to achieve your biggest dreams. Having meaning, knowing your purpose, and setting goals that align with these make a person truly unstoppable.

> **ACTION:** *Find mentors who are already doing what interests you. They can help guide you and will likely relate to any struggles you might have, especially in dealing with the comments of people who hold you back. Set your bar high, reach out to the very best people locally, and more importantly, globally. Be persistent and show commitment. You will be surprised at how many people will be willing to become your mentors if you just ask.*

ACTION: *Take opportunities to experience something new, especially those that allow you to travel. Gaining a new perspective on your own life and situation is always easier to do at a distance. A lot of people will tell you that their best business ideas came when they finally took time off from working. You don't need to go on holiday; going for a walk can provide immediate space from a current issue. If an opportunity is presented, take it. Too many people wait to have all their ducks in a row before they take action. The people who go the furthest from where they started usually take the opportunities even if they don't have all the details figured out.*

ACTION: *One way to experience gut reaction is in decision-making. Transformative coach Michael Neil suggests that when making a decision that seems hard, flip a coin and commit whole-heartedly to the action assigned to the side the coin lands on. If the coin lands and you immediately feel a gut reaction of "Oh no ... that's not what I wanted," then you now know, thanks to your gut response, what the right decision is. If your gut has an opinion, it's probably right!*

ACTION: *Finding our Why, the core of our motivations, the more profound meaning to our ideas, is made easier with the "7 Levels Deep" or "7 Whys" exercise. It is most effective if done with a friend.*

State your idea, or your feelings, or your current thoughts — whatever you want to go deep on — and then ask yourself the first Why? For example, it could be "Why is that important?" or "Why do you feel like that?" Once you answer the first why then you ask why again using the previous answer. You do this seven times. At some point, likely three or four levels down, you will go from answering from your head to answering from your heart. It takes a little work, but once you find your Why seven levels down, the revelation can be life-changing.

FINDING FLOW

At one point in my life, I was an outdoor activity instructor. Among other things, I would take clients kayaking down a river. We would start with a lesson on the riverbank so that people could learn the basics of paddling and the dangers to watch out for: how to steer, how to stop, what to do if the boat capsized … The most prominent danger would be tree branches (or full trees) that had been dragged downriver and left lying across rapids. Unlike what happens with rocks, the water could pass underneath and not have to change its course. The important thing was to keep a distance. If a kayaker could not stay clear and ended up capsizing, the key was to let themselves drift down the river until they came to a calm spot and could get out. Under no circumstance would you want to hold on to a branch as the water would end up going over your head and you would be at risk of drowning. But more often than not, capsized clients would immediately grab out for tree branches and end up needing to be rescued.

After the class, I would have everyone jump into their kayaks, and then I would push them into the river, and when the last kayak was in the water, I would follow after them. The novice kayakers would often go from shore to shore and even paddle upstream against the current. It would take a while to figure everything out, and in the process a lot of energy would be exerted. The trick was to get into the current and let it carry you downriver while you gently steered clear of any obstacles that might appear up ahead. And if you did capsize, all that was needed was to go with the current until it gently left you in a calmer area where you could get out.

Most people expect things to be tougher than they are and consequently overcompensate. Paddling upstream is a lot harder than just finding the flow. Once you merge into the flow, all you need to do is gently adjust your path to avoid unnecessary obstacles. And if you are challenged by an obstacle or rough section, know it is followed by calm waters. Life has a flow to it. You know when you are paddling upstream because everything feels like a lot of work. A small change in direction now can cause a wide variation to your future path, so it is best to make gentle corrections to your direction as you go along to stay in the flow.

ACTION: *Go river kayaking, and try to stay aware of how gentle the corrections are that you need to take to stay in the flow. Of course, there are many other activities that require gentle actions to keep us on the path. If you ride a bike, you can't make drastically abrupt and large turns or chances are you will get thrown over your handlebars. While driving, notice how gently the wheel needs to be turned for you to stay in your lane.*

ACTION: *Try to purposely avoid reacting drastically to hard times. Recognize that, as in a river, there are rapids and calm pools, and that there is always movement taking you downstream but the pace changes and the roughest waters can be the fastest to pass. What may feel like being out of control in your life doesn't last; sometimes you just need to surrender to the moment and trust that calm water lies around the bend.*

"I'm so focused...on everything!"

FOCUS

Our attention spans have diminished; we have an overload of information and give ourselves very little time to simply be. Due to technology, boredom seems a thing of the past. To be able to do our best work we need to be able to focus on the task at hand and eliminate all the mind clutter. If you take a step back from all of the goings-on in your life — your appointments, projects, jobs, obligations, emails, text messages, phone calls, activities, chances are you will realize that only a small percentage of them are things that truly bring you meaningful pleasure. The Collective and Shared Realities a lot of people experience would suggest being busy is a good thing. However, it is hard to be busy while being genuinely focused.

Finding your flow happens when you can focus strictly on things you love to do. I like to come up with a targeted list of the things I am working on and allow me to be focused. This list can be a daily micro list or a macro list for the month, year, five years. I call this the Magic List (see next section).

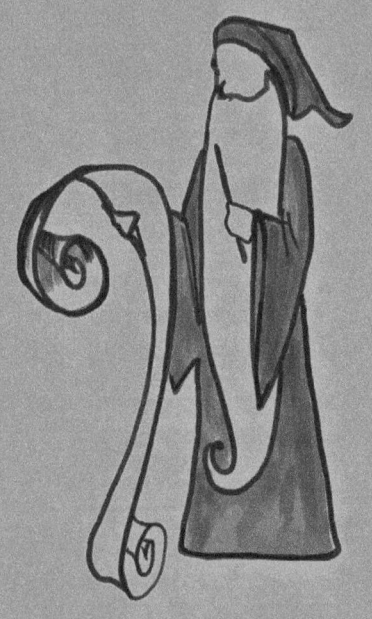

What's your Magic List?

YOUR MAGIC LIST

Although a lot of clients I have worked with are creative, something that consistently holds them back from achieving their goals is their own creativity. Being creative can mean having endless ideas, the ability to see opportunities and possibilities, and an ever-changing and evolving vision of your work and goals. This lack of focus can create two fundamental problems: (1) never being satisfied with your work and as a result holding it back from the public, and (2) having too many things on the go as everything becomes a possible project. Consequently, products don't get released on time and multiple projects on the go can spread a person too thin. (People who don't know what to do with themselves might think these are beautiful problems to have, with endless opportunities, possibilities and visions of perfection!)

Whether someone needs help in focusing their work or discovering their true calling, I like to suggest they create a "Magic List." The idea is to end up with a short list of only the things you genuinely want to do that provide you with the environment to perform at your highest level.

If you complete the Action at the end of this section, you should be left with a concise list of projects that will provide you with happiness, joy, meaning and money; allow you sufficient time to complete them in your designated time frame; enable you to apply your true value and most excellent attributes; and help you get in the zone, in other words concentrating at a level that brings out your best. This is your Magic List. Complete the projects on the list before you make a new one.

Keep in mind, "Rome wasn't built in a day, but they were laying bricks every hour." You need to ensure that your Magic List includes attainable short- and long-term goals. Don't overestimate what you can do in a day and don't underestimate what you can do in a year. Attempting too much in too short a time guarantees burnout and failure to reach your goals. Slow and steady does win the race.

Money is likely on your list of priorities. But I suspect that some of the projects you want to work on do not involve money, are not about money, or don't appear to have a clear path to generating revenue. At least one item on your list should not be attached to a financial goal. However, I believe that if you do excellent work, money will come with it. Business-related items on your list need to be making you money; if they don't, take them off the list immediately as they are just slowing you down from getting to where you want to be.

ACTION: *These are the steps for creating a Magic List:*

#1. *Create a list of all the projects and goals you are working on and those you would like to work on.*

#2. *Assign a number from 1 to 10 next to each project according to where it sits in order of interest and priority. Consideration for a priority should include: Does it make you happy? Does it bring you joy? Does it feel meaningful? Is it on your dream list? Does it make you money? Items that are not assigned a number of at least 7 need to be removed immediately. Remove any item from the list if it does not bring you at least one of the following: happiness, joy, meaning or money.*

#3. *Assign an amount of time each project will take to complete. You only have a finite amount of time, so be realistic about how long things will take to accomplish. Write a timeline with milestones. Remove all projects taking time away from completing on schedule the ones that matter.*

#4. *Create a list of the things you feel are your greatest talents and attributes, the areas where you bring the most value. Compare this list to the projects left after doing steps 1 to 3, and if any of the projects don't allow you to apply your greatest attributes and bring your true value, remove them immediately.*

#5. Write a list of what gets you in the zone, what puts you in your flow, what helps produce your best work. What circumstances provide the right environment? Think of examples of when you have felt in the zone; these could be incredible music performances, inspired art sessions, well-delivered speeches, clear decision making, extreme focus, high-level sports performances, a sense of happiness, contentment with the experience of the moment, a feeling of effortlessness, and so on. Compare this list with the projects left after steps 1 to 4. If there is a project on your list unlikely to provide you the opportunity to be in your zone, remove it immediately.

THOUGHTS & ACTIONS TO LIVE BY

Try to turn to this list often, and don't worry if you can only read a bit of it at a time.

- Recognize that your Personal Reality is an individual experience always seen from your perspective. Your version of reality is a unique experience.
- Acknowledge all your thoughts and feelings are your own. External circumstances are merely opportunities you can choose to react to as you see fit.
- Own your actions.
- Surround yourself with people you are inspired by, and benefit from their Shared Reality.
- Access information that builds on your own beliefs and the reality you are creating.
- Being cautious of what others say is wise as everyone is merely projecting their own Personal Reality.
- Be curious and open to possibilities you have not yet considered. The Collective Reality has shaped your idea of limitations.

Your THOUGHTS Create your Future

- Know that words are symbols carrying meaning far beyond the individual words written or spoken. Consequently, be selective of the words you speak to others and those you tell yourself.
- Don't be a victim of circumstance. Life doesn't do you wrong or right. You choose your perspective in your Personal Reality.
- Be mindful of your thoughts, the reactions they cause, and the actions they spark. Be mindful of your interpretation of the Shared Reality and Collective Reality. Be mindful of the reality you project onto others and perceive as theirs. You are always experiencing your Personal Reality.
- Perform to satisfy your personal reality, not the Shared Reality or Collective Reality.
- Do what you feel is right whether or not you think it is. (Listen to your intuition). Either way, it is all just a projection of your reality.
- Changing your circumstances is merely a matter of changing your perspective. You only have your Personal Reality, so look at things as you would like to see them. Know that you are already choosing your perspective.
- Recognizing that your Personal Reality is exclusively your own, that it is an entirely individual experience, is a giant leap toward metamorphosing into becoming a provider. From the moment you empower yourself with this perspective, you will always have what you need available to you. You will no longer be a dependant.

- Excuses are always made to yourself.
- Recover quickly from your negative reactions and instead turn your attention to positive actions.
- Your ability to reach your goals comes from within not from without.
- Meaning is inside of you; it does not come from Shared Reality. Finding meaning requires self-exploration. Self-exploration requires permission to be surprised by what you find. Permission needs to come from you, not from the Collective Reality.
- Fulfilment is a personal action.
- "Happiness comes when what you think, say, and do are aligned." (Gandhi)
- Focus and flow come when what you love and what you do are aligned.
- Keeping busy with too much on your plate guarantees stress and takes away from doing good work. Give yourself space, and you will gain clarity on what truly matters.
- Change happens instantly. It just takes time to get to the point of change.
- You can't achieve your dreams if you are losing energy building a Plan B. You only have an evolving Plan A in your Personal Reality.
- You can make an incredible impact on the Collective Reality. It is in the grasp of your Personal Reality to do so.
- Sometimes gaining a new perspective on your own reality can feel like standing in a bag and

trying to lift yourself up. It's impossible. In these cases, find a friend to help you see your situation through a new lens.
- Perspective is the lens you are looking through.
- Think. Believe. Do.
- Don't wait for change, make change.
- Take action immediately. If an action feels right, don't give it time to go from your heart to your analytical head. Just do it — five, four, three, two, one, go!

EPILOGUE

The way this little book should work is subconsciously. It has already found its way into your mind and is affecting your perspective. The things that have resonated, or possibly illuminated a light bulb or two, have now entered your perception of the world. Just the simple act of acknowledging something has an incredible way of affecting your actions, interpretations and experiences.

When I was in my early twenties, I used to get highly physical panic attacks. My whole body would shake violently out of my control. It affected me even wanting to leave the house. Not a cool experience. I went to see doctors, including specialists. Nonetheless, the attacks persisted for years, until one day I realized they were panic attacks. The moment that acknowledgment happened, the physical shaking went away, and it never came back, just like that. It took me a while to overcome the internal sensations that would still rise from time to time. However, the physical aspect ceased merely through acknowledging that I was having panic attacks. In the same way, information, especially that which we deem to be true

or that we are willing to entertain as being true, has an immediate impact on our subconscious mind.

I hope that at least some of what I have written will become true for you.

I wish you all the best.

Aaron Bethune

ACKNOWLEDGMENTS

Thank you to those that took the time to read this book and give me feedback early in its development, including, but not limited to:

Donald Bethune, Cheryl Cohen, Starlyn Cooper, Cory Friesenhan, Bob Guido, Jocelyn Hallet, Todd Harlow, Sarah Hook Nilsson, Clint Hutzulak, Adam Kerby, Suzi Khoury, Virginia McKenney, Cathleen McMahon, Spencer Mruk, Luke Ronse, Rick Salt, Ryan Stanley, Cherene Shea, and Colin Young.

A big thank you to my mother, Sarah, for reviewing the manuscript in detail and providing valuable suggestions. Another special thank you to my friend and editor, Cheryl, for her contribution.

I am very grateful to my parents, who shaped my thinking from an early age; the results are in this book.

Having children of my own has inspired me to think a little deeper and hopefully pass on some of my beliefs.

Last but not least, I am incredibly grateful to you, Laura, for always being supportive, believing in me, and for your beautiful illustrations that have brought this book to life. Thank you.

ABOUT THE AUTHOR

Aaron is an adventurer.

From climbing in the Andes and making records to speaking around the world and working with celebrities, musicians, entrepreneurs, charities, government, and corporations, Aaron is always excited to see life through a new lens and help others uncover a new perspective.

Aaron grew up in England and Spain and currently resides with his family in Canada's maritime province of Nova Scotia.

For more information, you can visit:
www.aaronbethune.com

To be in touch with Aaron directly, you can email:
aaron@aaronbethune.com

www.ingramcontent.com/pod-product-compliance
Lightning Source LLC
Chambersburg PA
CBHW061203070526
44579CB00010B/118